Original title:
Strawberry Hues

Copyright © 2025 Creative Arts Management OÜ
All rights reserved.

Author: Clara Whitfield
ISBN HARDBACK: 978-1-80586-396-0
ISBN PAPERBACK: 978-1-80586-868-2

Whimsical Drops of Lushness

In a garden of giggles, blooms take a dive,
Jesters in red coats, so bright, they arrive.
With a bounce in their step, they swish and sway,
Dancing in sunlight, just like a bouquet.

Plump and cheeky, they wink from the vine,
Whispers of sweetness in every design.
Chasing the bees, they play peek-a-boo,
A banquet of laughs, with a splash of dew.

Nectarine Sonnet at Twilight

At dusk, the orb shines on radiant cheeks,
Round fruits giggle softly, playing hide and seek.
Puns on their lips, they crack silly jokes,
While ants do the cha-cha, as if they were folks.

In this fruity frolic, the laughter flows wide,
Bouncing along with a bounce in their stride.
With a wink and a twist, the night takes its flight,
These plump little jesters dance into the night.

The Harvest's candy-coated Gift

Baskets brim full with cheeky delights,
Candy-coated blessings, oh what a sight!
With each perfect splash, they're sweetened just right,
A treasure chest bursting, a pure sheer delight.

Their playful demeanor, a frolicsome flare,
Swirling in midair, they waltz without care.
Each giggle and chuckle, a flavor so sweet,
Delightful connections in every heartbeat.

Cravings of the Heart's Orchard

In dreams of the orchard, they frolic and play,
With cheeky confessions, they brighten the day.
Little bursts of joy, the heart's favorite treats,
A juicy surprise with laughter that beats.

Sipping on sunshine, they savor each thrill,
Craving the sweetness, they can't get their fill.
With a wink and a nod, they pop off the tree,
Crafting a world of pure jubilee.

Raspberry Rain on Petal Paths

A drizzle of fruit, how absurd,
Tiny splashes on petals stirred.
Giggles dance with every drop,
As bumblebees in circles hop.

The roses blush with cheeky pink,
Do they dare to giggle or wink?
Bouncing raindrops on the ground,
Make puddles where laughter's found.

Silly clouds in a berry chain,
Seem to join the silly game.
Each petal's kiss, a laugh so spry,
As fruit rains down from cotton sky.

At twilight's call, a joke is told,
Petal paths gleaming bright and bold.
Upon this stage where we all twirl,
Raspberry rain makes the day unfurl.

Dolls of Berry Adornment

Dollies dressed in berry cheer,
With rosy cheeks, they twirl near.
Lopsided hats on tiny heads,
While giggles bounce on plushy beds.

A jester's raspberry grin so wide,
Bobby pins in a berry tide.
Cotton skirts and jelly shoes,
A dance of colors, who can refuse?

They spin and sway, the dolls take flight,
In their world of juicy delight.
Every leap, a wobbly show,
As laughter spills like jam, you know.

At day's end when shadows blend,
These silly dolls are quite the trend.
With berry charms on laughter's stage,
They keep us lonely folks engaged.

Sunlight and the Serenade of Berries

Sunlight filters, warm and bright,
Berries sing, oh what a sight!
The giggling leaves burst from the trees,
Their humor carried on the breeze.

A chorus of laughter, the vines entwine,
Cheeky fruits in a joyful line.
Under the sun, they bounce and play,
Fruity jokes lighten up the day.

A sing-along, the garden's jest,
Each berry adding to the fest.
With every bloom and every cheer,
The world is bright when berries near.

As evening draws, the laughter stays,
In the golden light, all sing praise.
A serenade of silly sights,
Where sunshine fades but joy ignites.

A Canvas of Summer's End

Summer's brush paints shadows long,
With quirky hues where we belong.
The fruit parade, all shades of fun,
As daylight whispers, "We've just begun!"

Laughter spills on fields of green,
The oddest sight, a berry queen.
With a crown of wild vines in place,
She twirls around with a goofy grace.

As colors mingle and play so bright,
Each sunset joke enchants the night.
When nature chuckles, we join in too,
Painting our world with laughter's hue.

Finale of summer, a gigglefest,
As we bid the season, it's best to jest.
In this tapestry, every hue blends,
Creating joy, where the silly never ends.

Petal-Pink Dreams on the Horizon

A cheeky sun peeks through the trees,
Where giggles float upon the breeze.
With every bloom that sways and bends,
Silly antics tease the bends.

A bouncy ball rolls down the path,
Causing laughter and sudden wrath.
Laughter bursts like bubbles, bright,
A dance of joy in morning light.

Ripe Moments in the Glade

In a clearing where fun's the game,
A squirrel chased its tail, oh what a name!
With acorns flying all around,
Nature's jesters in mischief abound.

The breeze plays tricks with silly hats,
As squirrels jump through pools of sprats.
Laughter echoes in leafy rooms,
While flowers chuckle, shedding blooms.

Flavors of Dusk and Dawn

As dusk spills colors on sky and ground,
Teasing shadows make silly sounds.
The moon whispers jokes to the stars,
While fireflies light up the night like cars.

Dawn arrives with a sleepy grin,
Underneath the laughter's din.
Coffee cup spills, not just a drop,
While toast turns tricks for a belly flop.

Blushing Secrets beneath Green Leaves

Under emerald canopies so lush,
Bugs converse in a silly rush.
They share secrets, a comic plot,
Swapping tales of the veggies they've bought.

Each leaf is a stage for playful sprites,
Whose giggles fill the starry nights.
With cartwheels 'neath the branches wide,
Nature's jesters in mirth abide.

Floral Ballet in Blushing Tones

Petals dance in rosy light,
Waltzing with the breeze in flight.
Bumblebees in tailcoat suits,
Catching nectar in their boots.

A ladybug joins the fun,
Twiddling legs, oh what a run!
With antlers high, the beetles prance,
In this silly summer dance.

The Lure of Eden's Lore

In gardens lush, a tale unfolds,
Where laughter blooms and mischief molds.
A jester swaps the fruit for stones,
Delightful chaos, giggles thrown.

Each berry laughs, a cheeky grin,
As worms declare, "Let's all jump in!"
With every squish, a prank to share,
In Eden's realm, we laugh and dare.

Melodies Bouncing on Berry Bliss

Tunes of cherries, sweet and bright,
An orchestra of pure delight.
The raspberries beat drums galore,
While blueberries strum by the shore.

Dancing toes on a grassy floor,
Oh, what joy, we cannot ignore!
Even the moon joins in the game,
Shining light on our giggling fame.

Whirls of the Ruby Wind

The wind whirls 'round with a giggle sound,
Twirling each berry, spinning them around.
A troupe of squirrels in their fun brigade,
Trying to catch the color parade.

With every breeze, a pie takes flight,
As pies argue over who's more right.
The cherry bombs make quite the scene,
In this playful world, so vivid, so keen.

Dappled Shadows in Red-Bright Glories

In a garden where laughter blooms,
Tiny critters suit up in costumes,
A rogue ant steals a juicy prize,
While frogs wear crowns and jesters rise.

The sunbeam dances on leafy greens,
Whispering secrets to all it means,
A grasshopper sings a merry tune,
While bees play tag beneath the moon.

The Secret Kiss of Horizon's Edge

At dusk the skies swirl like a treat,
Cherries nodding, they can't be beat,
Giggling clouds stretch with every gleam,
As fireflies flash like stars in a dream.

The horizon winks, oh what a sight,
Invisible promises held tight,
A twilight dance that twirls and spins,
As silly shadows play hide-and-seek wins.

Heartfelt Whispers of the Berry Patch

In the patch, the gnomes share wine,
Picking fruits, tasting the brine,
A rogue raccoon with a cheeky grin,
Steals the treats while sister spins.

The bushes sway with a chuckle loud,
Secrets hidden beneath the shroud,
A squirrel's party, snacks galore,
Finding crumbs, they dance and roar.

Rhapsody of Nature's Gracious Fruits

The fruit parade marches with flair,
Apples strut with comedic air,
Lemons giggle in citrus tones,
While plums toss confetti from their thrones.

Each berry bursts with laughter bright,
Reflecting joys in the soft moonlight,
A harvest ball with jests and play,
Nature's bounty brings the fray.

The Sweetness of a Sunset's Caress

The sun drops low, a juicy treat,
A sky of jam, so ripe and sweet.
Birds are dancing, what a sight,
While clouds connect the day and night.

A giggling breeze tickles my nose,
As evening's laughter gently grows.
The sun winks back, oh what a tease,
While shadows sway like jelly knees.

Luscious Landscapes at the Day's Close.

The hills blush red, a drippy scene,
With patches bright, like fruits they glean.
A squirrel prances, all chubby and round,
Chasing twilight, skipping the ground.

The grass hums tunes, a fruity hum,
While crickets join, a happy drum.
A picnic spread, a silly bunch,
End up with crumbs from a berry lunch.

Crimson Whispers of a Summer's Eve

The night is swirled in berry schemes,
Whispers float like sweetened dreams.
Fireflies blink, with cheeky grins,
Making mischief in the winds.

With giggles shared 'neath leafy shade,
A chorus sings of giggly trade.
What's left untouched, let's poke and prod,
Even the moon seems to nod and nod.

Sweet Serenade of the Berry Fields

In fields aglow with laughter bright,
Dancing petals in the fading light.
Bumblebees buzz with funny flair,
Making music from the zesty air.

A tart, sweet mess, oh what a fuss,
As children collide, creating a bus.
Nature's concert, a joyful roar,
With berry stains on every floor.

The Color of Sweetness

The fruit wore a bright candy coat,
Like a joke that just got a funny quote.
It danced on the plate like it owned the day,
With tiny seeds that wanted to play.

A splash of fun in every bite,
Tickling taste buds, oh what a sight!
The flavor's a prankster, bold and quite spry,
Leaving laughter as flavors fly high.

Juxtaposition of Red and Green

In a joke that's sweet, the colors collide,
Red giggles loudly, while Green tries to hide.
Like a clown in the garden, so full of cheer,
They argue and bicker; it's all quite unclear!

"I'm juicier!" boasts the red one with glee,
"Not without me, you wouldn't be free!"
They poke and they prod in this color parade,
A comedy sketch that never will fade.

Lush Fields of Berry Delight

In fields of laughter, the berries play sweet,
Rolling downhill on their tiny little feet.
They slip and they slide with giggles abound,
Chasing each other, round and round!

With every plop, a chuckle is heard,
As they race to the patch, oh what a herd!
This fruity escapade brings joy to the land,
A berry bash led by the funniest band.

A Symphony in Blush Tones

In a concert of colors, the blush takes the stage,
Notes of laughter weave through every page.
With melodies sweet, they chuckle and sway,
Creating a scene that just brightens the day.

Each bite a tune, each laugh on repeat,
As the notes of the fruit play a whimsical beat.
Harmony blooms in the garden so lush,
A musical jest, all wrapped in a blush.

Luscious Lull between Blossoms

In the garden, colors clash,
Fruits think they're in a bash.
Wobbling bushes, giggling leaves,
All while the buzz of humor weaves.

Bees with shades of mismatched stripes,
Dance around like silly types.
With a wink, they snag a bite,
Bumbling joy, what a sight!

When the Garden Blooms in Flame

Petals glowing, a fiery cheer,
Dancing bugs, now I see clear.
Twirling round, they lose their shoe,
Oh what fun, this garden view!

The sunbeams tickle, the fruits all quirk,
Cabbages waiting for their perk.
Laughter sprouts from every vein,
Nature's jesters, never plain!

Kaleidoscope of Garden's Abundance

Look at that fruit, it's wearing pride,
Caught in dance, an awkward glide.
Colors flutter, here and there,
Garden laughs, what a flare!

Raccoons juggling, grapes on their heads,
Squirrels gossiping in little beds.
This hullabaloo, a much-loved spree,
Nature's comedy, wild and free!

The Glimmer of a Berry's Heart

Once a berry, round and sly,
Planned a prank, oh my, oh my!
With a tickle and twist, it made a splash,
A fruit fiesta, a berry bash!

With stems awash in joyful cheer,
Laughter bubbled, loud and clear.
In this patch, the silly sings,
Comical worlds that nature brings!

Luscious Bouquets in Dappled Light

A fruit parade upon the vine,
With colors bright and flavors fine.
Tiny hats of sunshine glow,
Wobbling seeds that dance to show.

Bouncing berries, red and round,
Falling softly to the ground.
They giggle as they roll away,
In this sweet and silly play.

With every bite, a burst of cheer,
Juicy laughter is so near.
A whimsical delight afresh,
In nature's chaos, we enmesh.

So picnic spread with joyful glee,
On checkered cloth, just you and me.
Let's dive in with savor and zest,
In this fruity, funny fest!

The Essence of Juicy Days

A splash of red, a dash of fun,
Under the warm and glowing sun.
Like little clowns in green attire,
They tickle taste buds, never tire.

Jumping jests on breakfast plates,
With syrupy jokes that one celebrates.
From smoothies tossed to fruity snacks,
These merry morsels lead the packs.

Every nibble, a chuckling treat,
With giggles hiding, oh so sweet.
In every slice, a joke unwinds,
Nature's punchline, oh how it shines!

So cheer for days of pure delight,
Where laughter blooms and feels just right.
Let's sip the nectar, laugh and play,
In this essence of a juicy day!

A Symphony Carved from Nature's Heart

In orchards full of cheeky cheer,
The fruits conspire, bringing near.
A cacophony of pink and glee,
As nature's jesters, wild and free.

With every pluck, a comedic tune,
Under the laughter of the moon.
Fruity frolics in the fields,
As nature's hand our joy reveals.

Oops, a slip! A berry flies,
Laughing loudly at the skies.
Juicy jokes upon the breeze,
Nature's humor sure to please!

So join the song, let's dance and sway,
With every theft of bright array.
In this symphony, we take part,
Carved with love from nature's heart!

Glistening Abundance in the Field

In the sun's warm embrace, they play,
Dancing in breezes, bright all day.
With laughter that tickles the air,
Bouncing around without a care.

Round and plump, they can't retain,
Joyful giggles, pure, unchained.
They roll down hills with a cheerful grind,
Like bouncing balls, they're one of a kind.

Melodies of the Garden's Jewel

In the patch where mischief grows,
Singing sweetly, the laughter flows.
With a wink, they tease the bees,
Inviting them with playful ease.

Ticklish leaves share secrets grand,
While critters join in this fun-filled band.
Songs of joy from every vine,
In the garden, all is fine.

The Playful Paint of Earth's Canvas

Throw a splash of bright delight,
Colors dance in pure sunlight.
A silly game of hide and seek,
Wobbling cheeks, oh, how they squeak!

Artful spoons scoop up the cheer,
As vibrant giggles fill the air.
Each bite's a burst of sunny cheer,
Tickling taste buds, oh so near.

Berries Beneath the Soft Horizon

Chasing shadows, the fun devours,
Beneath the sky, they share their powers.
With a twirl and a mighty leap,
They bring the daylight out of sleep.

The sun dips low, a playful mark,
As colors wink from the dark.
In the twilight, laughter plays,
Berries shine in the soft, sweet haze.

Elegant Tints of the Glistening Garden

In the garden where giggles bloom,
Colors clash like a playful cartoon.
Petals dance in the breeze, so spry,
Bugs don bow ties as they pass by.

Sunshine spills in a bright parade,
Each flower grins in a masquerade.
Worms in tuxedos wiggle and play,
Who knew dirt could be this cliché?

Tulips gossip and daisies tease,
Nature's humor drifts on the breeze.
With each bloom, a chuckle is sparked,
A symphony of joy, lightly marked.

In this patch of whimsy and cheer,
Life's quirks make the garden dear.
For every petal, a grin so wide,
In colors where laughter can't hide.

The Palette of Sunset's Laughter

When the sun wears a vibrant crown,
Red, pink, and gold tumble down.
Clouds puff up like cotton candy,
As giggles paint the sky so dandy.

A cheeky breeze gives trees a shake,
Leaves whisper secrets for humor's sake.
Squirrels jive under the setting rays,
In a twilight dance, they wildly play.

As shadows stretch across the land,
Nature chuckles, a simple band.
Bathed in colors, a playful toast,
To giggles and dreams that we love most.

In this scene where laughter reigns,
The day is done, but joy remains.
With every brushstroke, a cheer arises,
In the evening's glow, bliss never disguises.

A Rhapsody Born from Nature's Love

In the meadow, where joy takes flight,
Bumblebees buzz, oh what a sight!
Flowers dressed in their finest glee,
Chortling blooms, come join the spree!

Petals flutter like tiny kites,
Pansies laugh in the soft twilight.
Butterflies waltz, a raucous crowd,
Each giggle whispered, shrouded in loud.

A parade of colors, no frown to find,
Nature's comedy, uniquely designed.
With every sunbeam, mischief anew,
In the symphony of colors, joy's in view.

As the crickets chirp their tiny tune,
Even the night blooms cheeky and June.
In this rhapsody, hilarity thrives,
Amidst the laughter, our heart feels alive.

Captured Dreams of the Earth's Fondness

In a world painted with playful delight,
Fields reign in colors, oh what a sight!
Dreams abound in each playful shade,
With giggles and whispers, the earth's paraded.

The squirrels toss acorns, a daring game,
While butterflies giggle, never the same.
Clouds morph into creatures that prance,
In this whimsical landscape, we dance!

Rainbows dip in puddles of cheer,
Each drop sparkles, a laugh to steer.
The sun and moon share a winking glance,
As night brings forth a soft, silly trance.

Every twig and leaf, a vibrant muse,
Nature's sweetness, all sorts of hues.
In this land of jests and playful schemes,
We capture laughter, fulfilling our dreams.

Sunkissed Treasures in the Orchard

In a sunny patch, plump fruits play,
Hiding behind leaves, they giggle all day.
Tiny hands reach, for nature's sweet treat,
Tickling my nose, oh, such juicy feats!

Baskets in hand, we race with delight,
Slipping and sliding, what a funny sight!
Laughter erupts, we tumble and roll,
Nature's bright gems bringing joy to the soul.

A Palette of Fragrant Delights

Colors collide where the wild things grow,
Painted with laughter, in bright, vibrant show.
Pies in our minds, we dream as we roam,
Baking disasters that smell like home!

With whipped cream mountains, the toppings galore,
Spreading the chaos, oh, what a score!
Friends come together, with forks in a fist,
Mocking the flavor that none can resist!

Harvesting the Warmth of July

Summer sun shines on a jolly parade,
With juicy fun feasts that never do fade.
Splattered and stained, our faces in glee,
As we dance in fields, oh, wild and free!

Bouncing about, in a fruit-filled delight,
Silly faces painted, what a funny sight!
Ice cream drips down, oh, what a big mess,
Wiping our cheeks, we can't help but confess.

Melodies Wrapped in Fuchsia

In a garden's chorus, the giggles resound,
Where plump little wonders bounce all around.
Songs of the orchard, with rhythm we sway,
Chasing each other in a bright, bouncy play!

With friends by our side, we twirl and we prance,
In a berry-filled frenzy, we join the dance.
Twinkling like stars, the sweetness displayed,
In laughter and love, joyfully unmade.

Gardens Overflowing with Warmth

In the garden, laughter grows,
A jester's hat full of bows.
Tomatoes blush in a shy dance,
While bees join in at every chance.

Cucumbers don shades of bright green,
Potatoes hide in a clumsy scene.
Carrots giggle beneath the ground,
Wondering why they're never found.

A Dance of Red and Gold

Dancing fruits in a playful whirl,
An apple twirls in a citrus swirl.
Bananas giggle, the cherries tease,
While lemons frown in the summer breeze.

Grapes roll by in a goofy spree,
Twirling round like they're at a spree.
A peach slips on its fuzzy skin,
And everyone bursts out laughing in.

Wild Fruits in a Sunlit Glade

In the glade where wild fruit thrives,
Tales of mischief come alive.
Blueberries trail like they're in a race,
While figs hide behind the leafy lace.

Blackberries bump and tumble free,
Tickling the bumblebee.
Elderberries spot a game of tag,
Each running off with a giggly brag.

Cherished Moments in Crimson Light

In the twilight, laughter glows,
As friends share snacks in a row.
Pies of red evoke a cheer,
Spilling crumbs both far and near.

Silly faces, whipped cream hats,
Dancing down to the quirky chats.
With each bite, the giggles bloom,
In the kitchen, we light up the room.

Crimson Whisper of Dawn

A berry thought, how very strange,
Thought it was sweet but felt deranged.
In the garden, I made a toast,
To all the flavors I love the most.

A squirrel in a hat, can you believe?
Stealing my fruit, oh, what a thief!
I giggled as he danced and pranced,
While I just sat, a little entranced.

In nectar dreams, I took a dive,
Wishing my jam would come alive.
With pockets full of sugary treats,
I ran from ants on tiny feet.

The day is bright, the laughter grows,
Playing games in a fruity prose.
As bubbles burst and laughter flows,
I cherish this, where mischief glows.

Scarlet Dreams in a Garden

In a patch of red, I took a seat,
Chasing giggles with my bare feet.
A ladybug, with swagger and flair,
Pretended to dance without a care.

I planted smiles in rows so neat,
Wishing on clouds, they smelled so sweet.
A gnome with glasses, quirky yet spry,
Started to talk like he could fly.

Oh, what a sight! The blooms all titter,
As worms in hats just chomped on litter.
I tried to catch laughter in jars,
But ended up with a garden of stars.

The sun sets low; shadows are fun,
Endless giggles in day's sweet run.
With every chuckle and clever rhyme,
I'll garden my joy till the end of time.

Rubies Beneath the Sun

Underneath the sun, I spy,
A treasure trove, oh my oh my!
Rubies glisten like silly jokes,
Tickling me, these fruity pokes.

A squirrel in shades, with snacks galore,
Bargaining berries, who could ask for more?
My basket bursts, what a sight to see,
With jellies and giggles, just you and me.

A feathery friend with a wild hairdo,
Cracked up when the sun started to stew.
"Hey! Where's your drink?" I called out loud,
He winked back, "With you, I'm always proud!"

The day winds down; laughter keeps score,
Counting joy 'til we can't take more.
In every twinkle and berry pun,
I've found my treasure—oh, sweet fun!

Blush of the Morning Bloom

Awake to blush, the world's alive,
In silly hats, the flowers thrive.
A bee with rhythm suddenly hums,
While I make funny faces at passing chums.

I found a petal, pink as a song,
Chasing giggles as I skip along.
With every step, the garden grins,
Whispers of laughter on cheeky winds.

Oh, the morning is one big jest,
Each blossom wears its very best.
With butterflies donning brilliant hues,
The jokes just flow like juice to booze.

So here's to blooms, both sweet and wild,
In a world where I'm forever a child.
With chuckles bright and a playful tune,
I'll dance with joy under the warm afternoon.

Vibrant Sketches of a Sunlit Dawn

In the morning light so bright,
Birds start their chatter, take flight.
Grass tickles toes, oh what a tease,
Giggles behind trees, carried on the breeze.

With pancakes stacked, syrup like glue,
A squirrel leaps in pursuit of a crew.
The sun winks down, a jester at play,
While shadows dance and cavort the day.

Jelly stains on cheerful shirts,
As laughter erupts and joy flirts.
A race with ants, who quicken their pace,
In this joyful chaos, we find our place.

The day rolls on, like a wheel of cheese,
Each moment we grab, with giggles and ease.
A canvas of colors, just like our laughs,
Painting memories, the best of our halves.

The Vine's Silken Embrace

Tangled vines in a silly dance,
Wrapped around like a clumsy romance.
Grapes giggle low, sharing whispers sweet,
As bees buzz around, tapping their feet.

Sunshine drips like melted cream,
Frogs croak their tunes, lost in a dream.
The garden's alive with a jolly parade,
As flowers pop out like laughs unmade.

Ladybugs wiggle in polka-dot suits,
Trying to flirt with dandelion roots.
A chubby old snail, moving with charm,
Calls out to flowers, 'I mean no harm!'

In this green kingdom of laughter and cheer,
Every playful breeze shouts, 'Come over here!'
With mischief afoot and giggles all round,
The vine's silken embrace is joy unbound.

Juicy Echoes in the Garden

Beneath the sun, where the laughter flows,
Carrots hide with their colorful clothes.
Tomatoes chuckle, red as a prank,
While parsley puns all over the rank.

Cherries bounce like playful dreams,
In a symphony of silly screams.
Cucumbers jump, looking oh so sly,
Waving hello as the bunnies hop by.

The radishes wear their hats quite low,
Sipping juice during the garden show.
Fruits sharing tales of their summer fling,
In a joyful chorus, all dance and sing.

With each silly juggling of ripe delights,
The garden erupts in laughter-filled sights.
Echoes of joy in the fruity land,
Where giggles and flavors walk hand in hand.

A Tapestry of Blush and Gold

In a patch of sunlight, colors collide,
Laughter sprinkles like confetti wide.
A blanket of blush, the bees take a dip,
While flowers sip nectar, a sugary sip.

Pom-pom petals pirouette with grace,
Making sure no one steals their place.
A dandelion puffs out, with a giggle bright,
Wishing on the wind, oh what a sight!

The sunbeams tickle, making shadows play,
As the breeze joins in on this silly ballet.
With giggles and chuckles, the fruits do shout,
'We're juicy and joyful, no doubt, no doubt!'

In this tapestry woven of fun and light,
Every stitch is a memory, a delight.
Whimsical wonders unfurl in the fold,
Crafting tales in hues of blush and gold.

Canvas of Lush Desire

In a field where colors splash,
The berries dance and twirl in a flash.
A bunny hops with a silly cheer,
Sipping nectar, oh so dear.

With every bite, a giggle erupts,
Juicy drips, oh how it disrupts!
A painter's palette on the ground,
Nature's humor all around.

Worms wear ties; they're quite a sight,
Hosting a party, what a delight!
With laughter loud, and silliness wide,
A fruit fest where fun can't hide.

Oh, the canvas of sweet delight,
Crafted under the sun so bright.
For every splash and every smile,
Nature throws a funny style.

The Embrace of Warm Sunbeams

Under rays that tickle and tease,
The fruits giggle in the gentle breeze.
A cat naps, dreaming of a feast,
While ants have parties, to say the least!

With every pounce, the sunbeams chase,
As birds sing songs of a comical race.
Dewdrops sparkle like tiny gems,
Guests at a picnic, alongside them!

Lush greens sway to a silly tune,
While flowers prance under a cheeky moon.
The whispers of nature, filled with jest,
As critters fashion a fruit-loving fest.

So let the warmth embrace you tight,
In this garden of giggles, pure delight.
Where sunshine and laughter intertwine,
A cheerful stage, by design.

Ruby Cascades in the Afternoon

A waterfall of sweetness flows,
Berry-shaped giggles in bright show.
Rushing down with a splashy cheer,
Making both fruit and friends adhere.

Frogs in sunglasses, sipping juice,
Complaining 'bout their silly truce.
With every drop, they croak a joke,
While snails slide by in a leafy cloak.

The sun plays peek-a-boo with ferns,
As butterflies dance, and the world turns.
A berry choir begins to sing,
In harmonies of love, each offering.

So savor this fruity afternoon,
Where laughter thrives and spirits swoon.
In ruby cascades, shimmer, and play,
Nature's funniest, bright cabaret.

Pinks and Reds of the Lowly Orchard

In an orchard bursting with cheer,
Pink and red fruits draw near.
Giggling branches sway and shake,
As critters plot their sweet escape.

A chicken wears a berry crown,
Strutting 'round without a frown.
While squirrels craft a berry bling,
Impressing all with their fruit fling.

With each pluck, a chuckle erupts,
As worms host a ball, their backs all up.
Under boughs of laughter spread,
A whimsical world where fun is bred.

So relish the charm in this lush green,
A place where giggles bubble and preen.
With pinks and reds in an orchard grand,
Life's laughter flows, hand in hand.

Nature's Juiciest Disguise

In the garden, wiggle and squirm,
A berry tries to catch a worm.
With all its seeds in a fine array,
It quips, "I'm not lunch, just here to play!"

The leaves chuckle in the breeze,
Whispers travel with such ease.
"Why sit still? Go take a dive!"
Said the fruit with a grin, feeling alive!

Squirrels giggle in the fray,
As they munch and bounce away.
"You can keep your fancy cake,
I'll just be the fruit that's great to take!"

With every splash of juicy cheer,
Nature shouts, "I'm just here, my dear!"
Why pick a song that's dull and gray?
Let's dance in circles, here we play!

The Aroma of Sun-Kissed Delights

Whiff of sweetness fills the air,
A fruit parade without a care.
Tiny critters gather 'round,
"What's that smell? Oh, that's profound!"

Buzzy bees start to cha-cha,
Dressed in stripes, a fancy gala.
With pollen pockets, they flit about,
Laughing, buzzing, without a doubt!

Beneath the sun, all things shine,
Fruit jests, "Hey, I'm doing fine!"
A splash of color on the vine,
Shouting, "Here's more fun, it's divine!"

With every drip and every drop,
Laughter echoes—never stop!
In nature's kitchen, a wild delight,
A feast for all, oh what a sight!

A Dance of Red Beneath the Sky

Under the sun, they twirl and spin,
Berries laughing, cheeky grin.
They leap and jump on the grassy floor,
Whispering secrets, wanting more!

A ladybug joined, thinking it grand,
"Can I join in?" she waved her hand.
"But first, make sure you're a goodly seat,
This dance is juicy, oh what a treat!"

The breeze, it tickles, and so they twine,
Round and round, in a vibrant line.
"Why stand still, let's shake our hue!
We're the berry club, just me and you!"

Crickets chirp in perfect time,
Hopping in rhythm, it's simply sublime.
In every jump and giggle shared,
In fields of color, no one is scared!

Threads of Ruby and Cream

On the vine, the colors clash,
A ruby jogger makes a splash.
With a wink, it pokes the cream,
"Join the fun; it's like a dream!"

Cream replied, "I'm soft and sweet,
But berries can't resist the heat!"
In every swirl, a laughter weaves,
"Who said we can't chase the leaves?"

Juicy giggles drip from leaves,
Crafting stories only nature weaves.
A colorful party, nothing too grim,
Pop the cork, let's all swim!

Messy hands and sticky bliss,
In nature's game, we can't miss.
With every snack and every cheer,
We dance in joy, let's persevere!

Sunlit Blush on the Wind

In a garden where giggles bloom,
The sun tickles plants in full plume.
Laughter dances, a playful breeze,
Berries giggle under leafy trees.

Awkward bees buzz, chase their own wings,
While ants parade, showing off their bling.
A plump little fruit wears a shy grin,
As it sips on the juice of sweet sin.

Raindrops rumble, a comedic show,
Slipping on petals, they put on a glow.
Nature chuckles, its colors so bright,
A scene so silly, it's pure delight.

Chasing shadows while touching the sky,
In this fruity folly, we all can fly.
So come take a trip, it's sure to amuse,
In the laughter of nature's sunlit views.

Delightful Harvest in Twilight Hues

Underneath the twilight's soft light,
Fruits gather round, what a silly sight!
They gossip and giggle, wearing their shades,
As bats start to swoop, unfurling charades.

With plump little faces, they loot the scene,
Laughter erupts, it's a fruity routine!
Chasing each other in ridiculous haste,
While squirrels look on, their treasure misplaced.

The moon starts to blush, out of pure delight,
As crickets tune up for a concert tonight.
Berries hold hands and waltz in a way,
That leaves us all rolling, convinced they can sway.

In the quiet of dusk, with a tiptoe of glee,
The scene wraps around, a sweet jubilee.
As laughter reverberates 'neath twilight's muse,
All join the fun, in delightful hues.

Dreaming in a Meadow's Glow

In a meadow where marshmallows float,
Animals gather, a comical coat.
A cow wears a cap, so mismatched and fun,
As popcorn clouds dance, oh what a run!

Little rabbits, dressed in bright pink,
Bounce around, making others rethink.
With a thumping of feet, they create such a fuss,
While birds make a choir, all laughing at us.

The daisies are winking, what a cheeky crew,
Each taking their turns in a flowery queue.
And the sun, like a clown with a bright silly face,
Claps for the daffodils—what a wild embrace!

Dreams are spun here, in the warmth's gentle flow,
Where giggles and colors are free to bestow.
So join the frolic, let laughter erupt,
In a meadow so bright, joy cannot be corrupt!

The Romance of Crimson Rains

When raindrops wear blush, it's a sight to behold,
Colors start dancing, they're brave and they're bold.
Splashing in puddles, they giggle and twirl,
Nature's own soap opera begins to unfurl.

Worms wobble about in their slippery shoes,
They throw a parade in this colorful ruse.
While frogs will serenade from their leafy retreat,
With each little leap, they never skip a beat.

Clouds play hard to get, feigning their tears,
As children run out, confronting their fears.
There's giggling and glancing, oh what a day,
While sky looks down, with a flush of dismay!

So if you hear laughter, amidst the rainfall,
Join in the chorus and heed nature's call.
For life keeps its secrets wrapped in silly chains,
In the romance of colors, under crimson rains.

Blood Ruby at Dusk

In the sky, a splash of red,
Like a fruit that's lost its head.
Wobbly clouds, a silly sight,
Floating like they're drunk tonight.

Chasing shadows on the ground,
While giggles echo all around.
A cat wears shades, it's quite absurd,
As if it thinks it's seen the world.

Laughter bubbles up with glee,
Even birds sing comically.
Mice on scooters race with grace,
In this madcap, wondrous place.

And just as twilight starts to fade,
A clown pops up, a grand parade.
With pies and laughs that fill the air,
Each moment's brighter, without a care.

Nectar of the Evening Glow

The sun winks down in a playful way,
Lemonade puddles where beasts dance and sway.
Fireflies wear hats and twirl around,
While moonlit giggles float off the ground.

A frog in a top hat tries to sing,
His croak, a charming, off-key fling.
Buzzing bees take the stage tonight,
Showing moves that are quite a fright.

Juicy drips from trees like fate,
Marshmallow clouds, we celebrate.
The wind's a rascal with tricks to share,
Whispering secrets without a care.

As time flows by, so sweet and bright,
We savor the nectar, pure delight.
Each chuckle rolls in warmth's embrace,
In this evening glow, find your place.

The Essence of Feathery Petals

Flowers giggle in the breeze,
Their colors popping like they're sneeze.
A butterfly dons a polka-dot tie,
Waving to a snail that's passing by.

Petals dance, a wobbly feat,
While ants serve snacks with tiny feet.
A ladybug tells the best of jokes,
Making even the daisies choke!

Bumblebees are pint-sized clowns,
Juggling their pollen as they bounce around.
The sun looks down with a hearty laugh,
Chatting with clouds in a comical half.

In this garden where chuckles bloom,
Joyful whispers echo, dispelling gloom.
Each petal's shade, a fun surprise,
A world filled with laughter under the skies.

Hues of Laughter and Love

Colors swirl with giggles bright,
As the moon prepares for the night.
With splashes of joy upon the ground,
Every fumble brings laughter around.

Dancing shoes made of gummy bears,
Skipping along with silly flares.
Noodles twirl in a graceful dance,
Creating a scene of pure romance.

Balloons escape in the softening light,
Carrying secrets, oh what a sight!
They tease the stars to come out and play,
As the world giggles, the night's on its way.

In hues where cheer and love collide,
Whimsical wonders, all joyfully glide.
So let's paint the sky with laughter anew,
In this colorful realm, just me and you.

Swaying in a Symphony of Color

In a field where giggles grow,
A fruit parade begins to flow.
The reds stand tall, the greens do sway,
As juice-filled dreams come out to play.

With every bite, a burst of cheer,
An orchestra of laughter, hear!
The berries tease with mischievous glee,
Turning mundane into jubilee.

Dancing rays of sunbeam light,
Fragrant whispers take to flight.
With nature's brush we paint the day,
In vibrant splashes, bright and gay.

Skip along this jammy ride,
Where sweetness and silliness collide.
Each smile a note, each laugh a song,
In this colorful ballet, we belong!

Delight in a Ripe Reverie

In a dream where giggles bloom,
Ripe wonders scatter all through the room.
A cheeky fruit with a funny face,
Winks and wiggles, oh what a place!

Pudding cups and frothy shakes,
Crimson drizzles, for goodness sakes!
The humor flows like spritz of cheer,
Each spoonful tickles, loud and clear.

Quirky colors, a joyous sight,
Happiness dancing, oh, what delight!
Nature's canvas, a playful parade,
Where juicy visions never fade.

Bouncing flavors swirl around,
In this fiesta, smiles abound.
With laughter ripe in every bite,
We savor moments, pure delight!

Elysian Pools of Flush and Flavor

Wading in sweetness, oh what a splash,
With giggles and grins, we'll make a dash.
Plump little treasures, a fruity delight,
Whispers of laughter, what a sight!

Dipped in syrup, they steal the show,
Juicy joy, and oh, how they glow!
Ever so tasty, mischief unfolds,
With every wink, a story told.

Mixing up giggles with festive cheer,
A candy-coated atmosphere.
We wade in flavors, deep and wide,
In these pools of fun, we take a ride.

Cheeky puddles, red and bright,
Drip and drop, a pure delight.
With each little splash, a message clear,
Life's sweet as laughter, let's give a cheer!

Lush Reflections of Nature's Palette

In gardens lush, a palette spills,
Crimson giggles above the hills.
Wiggly vines shimmy in the sun,
Painting the air with laughter, fun!

Colors collide in a playful dance,
Nature's jesters in a merry prance.
With chuckles bright, they blossom free,
Tickling toes like sweet-tart glee.

A party of flavors, oh so bold,
Merry stories waiting to be told.
The canvas of life, so wild and bright,
Where every hue brings pure delight.

Running through petals, feeling alive,
In this carnival, we jump and dive.
With each berry glance, a smile takes flight,
In nature's palette, everything's right!

Kissed by the Glow of Radiance

Beneath the sun's warm tease, we laugh,
A splash of red on nature's path.
Like candy blushes on the trees,
We dance in joy, a sweetened math.

With every bite, the giggles soar,
Juice drips down like summer's roar.
A quirky taste, a fruity score,
We share our treats, who could want more?

The bees buzz high with silly glee,
As we sip nectar's jubilee.
The world spins round, oh what a spree,
Nature's prank the best decree!

So raise a toast to radiant fun,
For every laugh, we've just begun.
In hues of joy, our hearts, they run,
Chasing moments, never shun.

Amongst the Brush of Sweetly Ripe

In gardens bright with splashes bold,
We giggle as the stories unfold.
A wild chase through leaves so green,
With berry treasures yet unseen.

We trip and tumble, oh what a scene,
The berries wink, they're roaring keen.
With every pluck, we burst with cheer,
Nature's candy, oh so dear!

Worms wear hats, they dance and prance,
As butterflies join in the dance.
A fruity feast upon our plate,
We laugh at fate, can it be late?

So here we hide beneath the sun,
Our berry dreams of silly fun.
Among the brush, we've just begun,
With laughter sweet, we've already won.

Luminous Threads of Nature's Story

In twilight's glow, we spin our tales,
With laughter weaving like the gales.
Each thread of gold, so gently tied,
A tapestry where joy resides.

The bushes shimmer, sparkling bright,
While critters plot their evening flight.
With every nibble, giggles bloom,
While we consume nature's lively fume.

A frolicsome feast, oh what delight,
As shadows dance, we take to flight.
Nature whispers in rosy tones,
Our hearts a-jump like springtime moans.

So join the whimsy, come and play,
In threads of laughter, we will sway.
With every chuckle, come what may,
In this wild tale, we'll find our way.

The Flavor of Timeless Enchantment

With every bite, a magic spell,
We taste the stories only we can tell.
A sprinkle of time, a dash of fun,
In flavors bold, we come undone.

The sunbeams giggle as we savor,
With laughter's dance, we find our flavor.
In juicy bites, the silly shines,
Like sparkling wine in happy lines.

The leaves are painted with comic grace,
While nature's critters join the race.
We leap and bound like silly sprites,
In this enchanted world of bites.

So let us sip on this delight,
With every crunch, our spirits light.
In timeless charm, we'll feel so free,
Where laughter reigns, just you and me.

Heartbeats Painted in Coral Sunshine

Under the sun, we laugh and play,
With rosy cheeks, we seize the day.
A berry hat dances on my head,
While silly ants steal crumbs from bread.

Chasing shadows, we bump and roll,
Our giggles echo, a joyful toll.
In fields of color, we prance around,
Painting life with love, laughter bound.

Sweet scents linger, a delightful tease,
We stumble through fruits, as if on keys.
Every bite brings a funny face,
A splash of joy, a playful grace.

Oh, the moments of splatted cream,
Laughter bubbles, a vibrant dream.
We dance with fruit, our feet in sync,
In this fruity world, we laugh and wink.

A Harvest Serenade in the Breeze

A basket full of jokes to share,
With fruits that smile, beyond compare.
In the orchard, we sing a tune,
While picking berries 'neath the moon.

Giggling as we pluck the best,
Our harvest anthem, a merry fest.
Each berry winks, they know the score,
We dive in laughter, and still want more.

Ticklish bushes poke at our sides,
As we tumble down, our laughter rides.
In nature's giggle, we lose control,
Beneath the branches, we find our soul.

A dance of sweetness in the air,
With every splash, we lose a care.
We write our stories on the ground,
In a harvest serenade, joy is found.

The Dance of Sweetness and Light

In a bowl of colors, a festival bright,
We twirl and spin, pure, merry delight.
Banana peels become our slides,
With each laugh, our joy abides.

Berries burst like fireworks high,
As we juggle fruits, reaching for the sky.
In this circus of nature, we play our part,
With smiles and giggles, we steal the heart.

A cherry on top of every joke,
While silly faces spark the poke.
Lemonade's laughter fills the space,
As we stomp and dance in a fruity race.

with each bright moment, we twinkle and wink,
Combining flavors, brighter than we think.
Amidst the fun, the sweet bites collide,
In this dance of sweetness, joy won't hide.

Emotions Brewed in Nature's Cauldron

A swirl of flavors and silly sights,
Nature brews laughter through day and nights.
We snicker at spills and splashes galore,
As fruit-faced gnomes knock at our door.

In whimsical gardens, we craft a stew,
With giggly grins in every hue.
Carved pumpkins laugh at the zany breeze,
Whispering secrets between the trees.

Cackling like hens, we dance in delight,
Under the stars, everything feels right.
A sprinkle of zest, a dash of cheer,
In nature's cauldron, happiness is near.

Slicing through laughter, we toss and we brew,
With giggles as bubbles, each moment anew.
In every concoction, joy gets its rise,
Brewing emotions, a feast for the eyes.

Fields of Lollipop Serenity

In fields so bright, I skip and sway,
With candy dreams that make me play.
The clouds are sweet like cotton fluff,
And laughter bubbles, oh so tough.

Gummy bears do dance on grass,
While licorice trees grow with sass.
I twirl around like a lollipop,
In this land where giggles won't stop.

Rabbits hop with jellybeans,
Wearing hats of whipped cream scenes.
A sugar breeze tickles my nose,
In a world where fun never slows.

With every step, my heart does sing,
A silly tune that makes me swing.
Fields of joy, come take a ride,
With gummy joy as my sweet guide.

Juicy Kisses of Summer Sun

Oh, juicy days, where sunshine glows,
With fruity laughter, everyone knows.
I chase the rays like a playful pup,
In this zesty world, I sip and sup.

The nectar drips from every tree,
As bees are buzzing, oh so free.
I wear a hat made of fruit salad,
In this realm where laughter's ballad.

A splash of juice as I take a dive,
In the sweet pool where giggles thrive.
The water's bright with cherry swirl,
In this summer's dream, I twirl and whirl.

So grab a slice and join the fun,
Under the bright and laughing sun.
With juicy kisses in the air,
This summer's laughter, beyond compare.

A Garden's Lullaby in Coral

In gardens bright, where petals dance,
A lullaby sings of chance romance.
The flowers chuckle as they sway,
In shades of coral, bright and gay.

Bumblebees with their buzzing jest,
Perform a waltz, it's quite the fest.
With every bloom, a joke is told,
As petals whisper secrets bold.

A snail in shades of candy pink,
Takes his time, but what do you think?
He wears a shell that's shaped like cake,
In this garden, laughter's not fake.

Oh, come and frolic with me, dear friend,
In coral dreams that never end.
With every petal, every leaf,
A giggle's promise, sweet relief.

When the Daydreams Turn Scarlet

When daydreams splash in scarlet hue,
The clouds wear smiles, and the sun says boo.
I chase the whims of silly sights,
As the sky twinkles with funny lights.

Butterflies with quirky flair,
Dance on breezes, light as air.
In my world of whimsy grand,
Every tiny thought is like a band.

The trees are giggling, oh-so-clever,
Sharing secrets, now and forever.
I pluck the stars like gumdrops sweet,
In a world where joy is a treat.

So join me in this playful chase,
Where laughter leaves a merry trace.
When dreams turn red, and spirits soar,
In this scarlet whimsy, we adore!

Juicy Secrets of Summer

Beneath the sun, we splash around,
A laughter burst, a squishy sound.
With every bite, the juice escapes,
Wearing red smiles on our silly shapes.

The ants parade like tiny kings,
While we concoct our berry flings.
A fuzzy hat? A sticky treat?
We dance around with sticky feet.

Slipping, sliding on the grass,
A challenge now, to have some class.
But who can stand in such delight?
We giggle, toss, and scramble — a sight!

So grab a bowl, let laughter flow,
In juicy seas, our joy will grow.
With rosy cheeks and sticky hands,
We form the best fruit-filled bands.

Rosy Reflections in Twilight

As day gives way to twilight glow,
We chase the sprites, put on a show.
With berry crowns and shoes of brown,
We twirl around, not gaining ground.

The squirrels chuckle, burry treats,
While we dance to our silly beats.
Our laughter ripples, hits the stars,
And so we dream of berry jars.

Oh, what a sight, our berry splash,
With nightly wonders, a fizzy clash!
We paint the sky with brightened cheer,
As rosy whispers fill the sphere.

And when the moon pops in to play,
We burst in giggles — hip hooray!
For nightly joys and fruity glee,
We toast our hearts, just you and me.

Berry Kisses on the Breeze

Whispers of summer, a cheeky tease,
Fragrant laughter rides the breeze.
With handpicked treasures, we roam free,
Canberry kisses? Oh, let's agree!

Splat! A berry aims for my nose,
As giggling friends erupt in prose.
We roll and tumble, blend and mash,
In our own world, a berry bash!

The sun dips low, we wipe our stains,
Brightened faces, skipping gains.
With every sip, our giggles rise,
A dainty laughter fills the skies.

So let's collide, be fruity, bold,
With berry tales that must be told.
With whispers sweet and laughter loud,
We weave a dream — let's gather 'round!

Petal Stains on the Sky

Painted petals on our hands,
We sketch our dreams with glitter bands.
Our laughter drips as colors blend,
Creating laughs around each bend.

Twirling petals in the air,
A sprinkle here, a giggle there.
With berry juice on every face,
We dance in bold, delightful grace.

The sun dips low, we paint the night,
Where every giggle feels just right.
With berry powder on our toes,
Our joyful hearts are sure to glow.

Through twilight hues and giggles bright,
We splatter joy on starry nights.
So take my hand, let's fly away,
With petal stains, we'll laugh and play.

www.ingramcontent.com/pod-product-compliance
Lightning Source LLC
Chambersburg PA
CBHW051732290426
43661CB00122B/237